THE

META

PLAYS

ANDREW BISS

ENTR'ACTE
EDITIONS

"The play was a great success, but the audience was a disaster."

— Oscar Wilde

It's Act 2, Scene 3 in another night's performance of a less-than-riveting romantic drama. As the two young leads navigate their turgid love scene, employing all their dramatic skills in an attempt to breathe life into their two-dimensional characters, another, far more gripping story is unfolding just beneath the surface. Despite a mutual loathing of each other, a devotion to the craft ensures that the show will go on; but the inner dialogues that play out inside each of them reveal a far different narrative than the one being played out on the stage.

The playwright creates the first character of his new play, but soon after the entire process grinds to a halt. As time marches on and the play continues to stagnate, the character's patience begins to wear thin. As frustration turns into animosity and antagonism, the playwright begins to realize that perhaps this is one relationship that was never meant to be. But what's a writer to do?

THE SKEWED PICTURE

1M/1F Approx. 10 minutes – Page 25

Bob and Betty have settled in for a quiet night at home. That is, until Bob makes a startling discovery that has the potential to reshape their entire existence…or at least their living room. The realization that a parallel universe could be staring them in the face forces them to question just who exactly these people might be, and more importantly, why they're there?

FILLER

1M/1F Approx. 15 minutes – Page 39

Two characters come to realize that the extended scene written for them in the middle of the play has no intrinsic value, does nothing to propel the story forward, and to all intents and purposes is completely extraneous. Their raison d'être pulled from under them, can they still maintain their credibility and sanity through several pages of what's little more than…filler?

THE CURIOUS ART OF CRITIQUE

2M/1F Approx. 15 minutes – Page 53

When reaction to his work on a new drama appears tepid at best, the director decides he must tackle the problem head-on and root out whatever it is that's leaving the audience unmoved. One way or another, the evening seems destined to end in tears.

WHAT'S THE META?

2 Any Age/Race/Gender Combination
Approx. 10 minutes – Page 67

Two written parts wait to be brought to life on stage. One of them, however, is found to be mired in a crisis of self-worth due to the size and quality of their role. The larger, more developed part must then attempt to convince its smaller counterpart of just how necessary they both are to the production that is soon to begin, and of the true and indisputable collaborative nature of theatre.

A REBEL AMONG THE WRETCHED

1M/2F Approx. 10 minutes – Page 81

A celebrated, multi-award winning dysfunctional family drama continues to enthrall audiences night after night. But what happens when one of the characters finally decides they've had enough doom and despair and resolves to leave the play to join…a musical?

TACKED-ON ENDING

1M/1F Approx. 10 minutes – Page 95

It's the end of the evening and two actors pack up their belongings and prepare to leave the theatre. While one of them felt the show went great, the other is left with the uneasy feeling that the final scene didn't quite deliver. Was his performance to blame, or was it the play's deus ex machina, which is not only highly implausible but also oddly familiar?

About the Author

Page 107

THE CRAFT

THE CRAFT

CHARACTERS

ACTOR 1: A cocky, bravura exterior masks the frustrated, insecure actor within. Male. 20s/30s.

ACTOR 2: Centered, professional, committed to her work, with an aversion to suffering fools. Female. 20s/30s.

SETTING & TIME

SETTING: A stage.

TIME: The present.

Playwright's note: This play contains very little 'actual' stage direction, as almost all of it is revealed by the actors themselves through their spoken inner dialogues. It should also be noted that since the dialogue in this play consists entirely of the actors' inner dialogues, neither of them at any time is actually hearing what the other is saying. Furthermore, both actors should – as far as possible – attempt to match their expressions and body language to what is being experienced by the characters in the play-within-the-play, rather than reflecting the emotions of the actors' inner dialogues.

At rise: There is a small table placed downstage center, with a chair to the right of it, and a small bench seat to the left. ACTOR 1 enters.

ACTOR 1: Act Two, Scene Three. I enter from stage right...nervous but in character, cross to the chair placed downstage center, next to the small table, and sit. I look up, seemingly forlorn, and begin my brief soliloquy that speaks of the turmoil and heartache inside of me that was all-too-obviously telegraphed in the previous scene. (*Beat*) I direct it to the fourth wall, as if speaking to anyone and no one, *and yet*...some woman in the third or fourth row is wearing a blouse of a color so loud and garish that I find my peripheral vision is being constantly distracted by it, thus diminishing the gravitas of what I'm attempting to impart to the audience at large. God I hate her – she's really screwing this up for me. (*Beat*) I ignore her as best I can and concentrate on the words. Okay, I'm done. God, I hate her – she really threw me off. (*Beat*) I think my expression at the end really got them, though...despite the distraction of Coco the Clown in row C or D or wherever the hell she is. (*Beat*) All right then, darling, let's be having you...make your entrance please...*now*. (*Beat*) Christ, where is she? Come on, come on! (*Beat*) All right, don't panic. Try to look deep in thought, as if there's a very important inner dialogue raging inside of you – then maybe the audience will think it's all deliberate. (*Beat*) God, I could strangle her right now! *Where the hell is she?*

(*ACTOR 2 enters from stage left.*)

ACTOR 2: I enter hurriedly from stage left.

ACTOR 1: *At last!*

ACTOR 2: I run across the stage, desperately seeking the whereabouts of my one true love...even though I can see him sitting right there and would have to be half blind not to have spotted him immediately...*but*...this is theatre, so on I search, hoping, hoping, until...oh yes, there he is...my heart's desire...in the form of one of the most obnoxious and egotistical jerks I've ever had the misfortune of working with. I smile sweetly.

ACTOR 1: I suddenly become aware of her presence...and of the very dark circles under her eyes, which no amount of make-up was able to disguise, apparently. Out on the town with the director again last night, I'm assuming. My, what a far cry from the delicate little flower she's attempting to fob off on the audience right now. Drunken old slattern. I turn away, hurt.

ACTOR 2: I drop to my knees and beseech him. If he only knew why I had to rebuff him in the library in the previous scene. If he only knew of the deep dark secret I've been forced to keep hidden from him. If he only…if he only…if he'd only look me in the eye for just a second! I mean, come on, we're supposed to be doing this thing together. It's called acting. It's reacting as well as speaking, you know? I need something to work with here. Hello? Hello?

ACTOR 1: I wonder if there's any agents in the audience tonight. I invited six but none of them responded. Wait a second…that guy back there with the glasses looks like he might be. (*Beat*) On second thoughts, no…too hip. Useless bastards. I expect they were all "too busy." Yeah, too busy propping up some bar, getting wasted after a hard day's skimming cash off the backs of their clients' hard work. Parasites. They should be sat out there doing their job…scouting for talent…witnessing art. (*Beat*) Oh, look out – her big speech is about to end. And not before time. She milks that thing like a Jersey cow. (*Beat*) I look up at her with a mixture of pity and confusion, and demand that she tells me her deep dark secret so that I can feign shock and surprise for yet another evening.

ACTOR 2: Oh look, it does have eyes after all. Good evening and thank you for joining me. It's so nice to have company. So…you want to know my terrible secret, do you? All right, I'll tell you. It's an almost uncontrollable desire to see you stripped naked and strung up by your balls from the light rigging, with a large prop of my choosing rammed up that vain, self-important and utterly talentless asshole of yours. But…since that's unlikely to transpire and not actually in the

5

text, I suppose I'd better stick with the scripted version. (*Beat*) She covers her face with her hands, dreading his reaction to what she is about to disclose.

ACTOR 1: Yes, cover it up, dear – it's hard staring into those dark, puffy eyes for too long. I feel like I'm sharing a scene with a panda bear. (*Beat*) And if there *are* any agents out there tonight, I hope they're taking note, because *this* is acting. Not only am I having to navigate this scene alone with Ling-Ling here, but I mean, really – she had an abortion two years ago after a brief romp in the rhododendrons with the former gardener? I mean, who writes this crap? I'm supposed to be shocked and appalled by this revelation? It's hardly the stuff of Grand Guignol. Now, if she'd been raped by her father and given birth to a hideously deformed, inbred monstrosity that she kept chained to a post behind the summerhouse, *then…then* we'd have a revelation…*then* we'd have something to work with. But no, it's just your average, plain vanilla abortion saga, in response to which – and to great effect, using every skill at my disposal – I fix her with a steely gaze that betrays neither outrage nor compassion.

ACTOR 2: I pause briefly, looking into his eyes to see if my words have been met with pity or loathing. (*Beat*) As it turns out, it's neither. It's that same vacant, idiotic expression he wears every time the director gives him a note – he tries to pretend he's understood, but in truth just looks lobotomized. And his parents, with the benefit of hindsight, would probably agree with me now that that might have been the best option. (*Beat*) I express lots of guilt, etcetera, and explain how my father forced me into it.

ACTOR 1: An abortion? I'll tell you what an abortion is – this script. Hard to believe it got a first production, let alone a revival. I should be doing Mamet or Pinter or Shepard, not this potboiling drivel.

(*Pause.*)

ACTOR 2: Oh Christ, he's forgotten his lines – and *always* at the same spot.

ACTOR 1: If I had an agent I wouldn't have to do crap like this. I'd get the roles I deserve…meaty ones…in juicy scripts…not this crap.

ACTOR 2: He has – he's forgotten his lines again!

ACTOR 1: God, I hate agents.

ACTOR 2: God, you *idiot!*

ACTOR 1: Useless bastards.

ACTOR 2: Think, you *idiot*, think!

ACTOR 1: Wait a second – where are we? Oh shit, it's my line!

ACTOR 2: *Think!*

ACTOR 1: Um…um, um, um, um…oh yeah – the very sudden, very clunky, not to mention plot-convenient change of heart, where I quickly forgive all and reaffirm my undying love. Urgh!

ACTOR 2: *At last!* I could slap you sometimes, I *really* could.

ACTOR 1: As if anyone could ever love that…apart from another panda, I suppose.

ACTOR 2: Amateur!

ACTOR 1: Oh, and the director, of course…after he's had a few.

ACTOR 2: Tears of joy fill my eyes, as I cross stage left to the window and look out, as if to symbolize the new life and new beginning that now lay ahead. Hackneyed and cheesy, yes, but that's what's in the script, so that's what I must do.

ACTOR 1: I cross to her and grab her by the throat. (*Beat*) Heh, heh, heh – just kidding. I tap her gently on the shoulder.

ACTOR 2: I turn around, my heart overflowing, to face my dear true love. My dear, true, lobotomized-looking love.

ACTOR 1: I get down on one knee, and from my pocket I produce a small box.

ACTOR 2: My eyes light up. Could it be…could it truly be…

ACTOR 1: Empty?

ACTOR 2: Oh shit!

ACTOR 1: Oh no!

ACTOR 2: You complete moron!

ACTOR 1: I swear it was there earlier. I swear it was. I checked…I think.

ACTOR 2: All right, don't panic, you idiot, just mime it.

ACTOR 1: Maybe it fell out. Maybe it's in my pocket. Perhaps I should check. No, I can't – the audience would know for sure then – it'd be obvious.

ACTOR 2: Just *mime* it.

ACTOR 1: What am I gonna put on her finger?

ACTOR 2: *Mime it!*

ACTOR 1: I'll just mime it.

ACTOR 2: He slips the engagement ring onto her finger, which she then lovingly admires – whilst deftly using her other hand to block its view from the audience – and proceeds to tell him how her heart is full of…well, actually, a death wish at this point.

ACTOR 1: That was quick thinking. The audience didn't suspect a thing. See, I don't panic in a crisis. That's the mark of a professional. You're learning from the best here, Ling-Ling.

ACTOR 2: Which now brings us to the sadly inevitable – the moment in the play that tortures my mind and churns my stomach eight times a week…the kiss. She turns her head to one side, coquettishly.

ACTOR 1: All right, Olivier, eat your heart out. I hope you're watching, wherever you are, because this, my friend, is the highest mountain an actor has ever had to climb. This is what separates the men from the boys, the hams from the Hamlets, for this is the moment where – after summoning every last ounce of strength and courage – I am called upon to…lock lips with bamboo breath.

ACTOR 2: Make it convincing, but make it *quick*.

ACTOR 1: I am fearless. I am an actor. I can do anything. Even this. He grabs the furry beast by its shoulders, making his intentions unmistakable.

ACTOR 2: She appears coy and vulnerable, her lower lip quivering slightly in anticipation of what she knows is to come. Her stomach, on the other hand, is gripped by nausea and revulsion…her head by a duty to the craft.

ACTOR 1: All right, Ling-Ling, here I come. And there'd better not be any director residue left on those lips – from his mouth or otherwise.

ACTOR 2: Bracing herself, she doggedly repeats her mantra: It's Jude Law, it's Jude Law, it's Jude law, it's Jude–

> (*They kiss for several moments, before ACTOR 1 releases ACTOR 2 from his embrace.*)

ACTOR 2: …Law.

ACTOR 1: Done! He emerges unscathed, and yet another night's meager wages are earned in full. They should give medals to some actors, not awards. (*Beat*) He stands before her with a look of pride…as well he should after that feat.

ACTOR 2: She strokes his cheek affectionately…while resisting the overwhelming urge to wipe her mouth with the back of her hand, and imagining the poor creatures that have had to endure that revolting experience in real life…assuming there's actually been any.

ACTOR 1: He takes her hand and leads her stage right to the bench seat.

ACTOR 2: Why is he going so damned fast? The director's told him about this *so* many times! I'll trip and break my neck one of these days.

ACTOR 1: He gestures for her to sit.

ACTOR 2: She sits.

ACTOR 1: He sits and places his arm around her…and proceeds with the cloying speech about his plans for their future together, and how happy they'll be, and of the children she'll bear him…literally, in this case – half-man, half-bear.

ACTOR 2: She leans her head tenderly against his shoulder…and contemplates the true meaning of paying ones dues, knowing that one day…one day, when she's a sought after actress of fame and repute, all of this – every last unctuous, frustrating, degrading moment she's ever had to endure – will all have been worth it.

ACTOR 1: He holds her close to him…and waits impatiently for the lights to come down. (*Beat*) Wait a second…did I turn my lights off when I pulled in here tonight? Oh no…I don't think I did. Oh shit…*shit!* Hurry the hell up with those damn lights, will you? I've gotta get out of here *now!* Come on, come on!

ACTOR 2: Thank God he gets murdered by my father in the next scene. She smiles contentedly…as the lights fade down…to black.

END OF PLAY

A FLAWED CHARACTER

A FLAWED CHARACTER

CHARACTERS

CHARACTER: A character in a play.

AUTHOR: Playwright of the aforementioned play.

SETTING & TIME

SETTING: A stage.

TIME: The present.

At rise: CHARACTER is discovered sitting at a table, head nestled in arms atop the table. On the other side of the table are a pen and a pad of paper. The chair opposite is empty. Presently, AUTHOR enters and sits down in the empty chair.

CHARACTER: (*Head raised from repose*) Well, well…the great author returns.

AUTHOR: So it would seem.

CHARACTER: I'd all but given up on you.

AUTHOR: I told you I'd be back as soon as I could.

CHARACTER: I thought you said you were going to the bathroom.

AUTHOR: I did.

CHARACTER: Oh. (*Beat*) Problems?

AUTHOR: I don't think that's any of your concern or a particularly appropriate question to ask. But since you have – no.

CHARACTER: I didn't mean intestinal ones; I was referring to the creative variety.

AUTHOR: Oh. (*Beat*) Well, the answer's still no. I simply became sidetracked by…by some other matters that…required my attention.

CHARACTER: I see. (*Beat*) Of course, in my day we called it procrastinating.

AUTHOR: What do you mean, "In my day"? You don't have a day. I just made you up. You're a character I created for my play, that's all.

CHARACTER: All right, all right, scratch that. Forget I said it.

AUTHOR: You *didn't* say it. Until I write it, you haven't said it.

CHARACTER: Oh, excuse me. I stand – sit – chastened and corrected.

AUTHOR: Good.

CHARACTER: After all, you're the one with the pen.

AUTHOR: Yes I am, and don't you forget it. (*Brandishing the pen*) This is mightier than the sword, remember?

CHARACTER: Yes, well, whilst I appreciate the metaphor,

personally I know what I'd rather be holding if challenged to a duel.

AUTHOR: Well, since I have no intention of including any duels, you don't have anything to worry about, do you?

CHARACTER: No, I suppose not. But if I were wielding a sword against some poor gimp holding a ballpoint pen, I don't think I'd have been particularly worried to begin with.

AUTHOR: Look, can we just forget about duels? There aren't going to be any. In fact, there'll be no violence of any kind in this work.

CHARACTER: No...nor much of anything, really.

AUTHOR: Excuse me?

CHARACTER: Well, what have you got so far?

AUTHOR: (*Hesitates*) You.

CHARACTER: Yes, of whom we know nothing.

AUTHOR: Not yet, because it's...I've...it's just the beginning.

CHARACTER: And where's it going?

AUTHOR: What?

CHARACTER: The story. I mean, presumably there is one?

AUTHOR: Of course there is. It's a...it's a...a journey. A journey of which you will be a part of to some degree. Though to what degree I haven't yet decided...but it's getting smaller by the minute.

CHARACTER: So's your play.

AUTHOR: Look, I told you, it's just the beginning. It…it hasn't found its rhythm yet.

CHARACTER: Mmm…well, the play may not have, but you certainly seem to have hit your stride.

AUTHOR: Meaning what?

CHARACTER: Meaning the constant up and down from this table every five minutes. You're like a damn yo-yo. First it's the dog that needs walking, then it's the laundry that needs folding, then it's the sound of some God awful soap opera I can hear blaring from the next room, then it's some uncontrollable urge to dust the mini blinds – it's never ending. Meanwhile, I'm just sitting here not knowing who I am or where the hell I'm going.

AUTHOR: Join the club.

CHARACTER: It's all so static, don't you see? It's completely static. This play is going nowhere fast.

AUTHOR: You can't rush the creative process.

CHARACTER: But give me something, can't you? I need something to work with here. I need to *be* someone. For the love of God, flesh me out a bit!

(*Pause.*)

AUTHOR: The problem is…I'm not sure that I like you anymore. I've a feeling that may be the problem.

CHARACTER: Oh, give me a break, this isn't a popularity contest! *It's a play!* You don't have to like everyone in it. In fact, you shouldn't – it would be boring – which frankly, right now, this is!

AUTHOR: You see, when I first wrote you down, I thought we'd go somewhere together. I didn't know where, but I thought we would. But it doesn't seem to be happening. *(Beat)* Perhaps this just wasn't meant to be?

CHARACTER: Now you just listen to me. I have sat here patiently while you've made every effort to do anything and everything except follow through on what you started. I've stared into space, I've yawned, I've twiddled my thumbs, I've even – in my excruciating boredom – tried very hard to imagine a life for myself out of my own head. But I can't. Only you have the power to do that. So for the love of God, do it!

AUTHOR: I'm sorry…I don't think that I can. I think this may all have been a big mistake. I think, perhaps, I should start again.

CHARACTER: Don't you dare!

AUTHOR: It's not you, really it isn't.

CHARACTER: You just said it was.

AUTHOR: No, it's me, I…I should never have thought of you.

CHARACTER: Well, unless I'm missing something, you hardly have, have you?

AUTHOR: No, not a lot. But just enough, I suppose…to be too much.

CHARACTER: Oh, you *really* know how to make a person feel good? What a charmer. I'd just *love* to sit down and have dinner with you sometime. *Jesus!*

AUTHOR: It's nothing personal.

CHARACTER: I wouldn't know – I was never made a person.

AUTHOR: Well…probably for the best.

CHARACTER: Oooh…you really are a piece of work, aren't you?

AUTHOR: All I meant was–

CHARACTER: I know exactly what you meant, you supercilious, self-important, self-pitying, self-indulgent, self-aggrandizing…self! You think you're so high and mighty, but let me tell you something – one day…one day, when you're lying on some cold, hard park bench, stinking of piss and coughing up snot, I'll be there. I'll be there, and I'll be laughing; laughing *so* hard. Laughing and clapping and dancing and singing and celebrating everything that makes you utterly disgusting yet still cling to life because you don't have the guts to kill yourself.

(*Pause.*)

AUTHOR: And this little tantrum was intended to do what? Change my mind?

CHARACTER: No…just make me feel better.

AUTHOR: Did it?

CHARACTER: Somewhat.

AUTHOR: It doesn't change anything.

CHARACTER: There's precious little to change.

AUTHOR: My mind's made up. I'm sorry it had to be this way.

CHARACTER: Wait! Wait!

AUTHOR: What?

(*Pause.*)

CHARACTER: Just give me another chance. Think about me a bit more. Focus on me a little harder. Maybe…maybe things will start clicking. Maybe you'll find hidden depths to me – sides of me you never imagined were there. And before you know it, I could be kick-starting your imagination into producing something magnificent. Something game-changing. Something that shifts your career – such as it is – to a whole new level.

(*Pause.*)

AUTHOR: I don't think so.

CHARACTER: (*Hissing*) *You don't think so?*

AUTHOR: No. You're just not doing it for me. Let's face it, you're a non-starter.

CHARACTER: *Me! Me! I'm* the non-starter? Oh, you have some nerve, mister, you have *some* nerve. My God, the audacity! I think it's high time you took a long, hard look in the mirror, buddy. Then you'll come face-to-face with the real non-starter around here. You prance around this place like some pretentious dick-on-a-stick, thinking you're *so* artistic, and *so* literary. "Look at me, I'm a writer." "Look at me, I'm a playwright; I'm so *intellectual*; I'm so *esoteric*; a struggling, penniless martyr to my art." "I go forth like Quixote, noble and proud in the face of the doubters and non-believers, and do it all with my head held high and a fountain pen rammed up my precious, tortured ass!"

AUTHOR: You have *no* right to speak to me like that!

CHARACTER: But what do you really do, *really?* Not much of anything, really. You just like to *think* you do.

AUTHOR: Stop it!

CHARACTER: Because it makes you feel *important*. It makes you feel like you *matter.*

AUTHOR: I said, stop it!

CHARACTER: But guess what? News flash – *ya don't!*

AUTHOR: Enough!

CHARACTER: Hate to break it to ya, buddy – but ya ain't curin' cancer here.

AUTHOR: I'm warning you!

CHARACTER: Hell, you're not even writing a lousy play.

AUTHOR: All right, that's it! This is the end.

CHARACTER: What?

AUTHOR: I refuse to be spoken to like that by someone who *I personally* brought into being.

CHARACTER: You know, for a second there you sounded just like my father.

AUTHOR: You don't have a father. You don't even have a backstory.

CHARACTER: I was pretending.

AUTHOR: In fact…I've decided to make you an orphan.

CHARACTER: No!

AUTHOR: Yes. An orphan. Not only that…an orphan with a deadly and incurable disease.

CHARACTER: So it's a *tragedy*. *Now* we're getting somewhere.

AUTHOR: One of us is.

CHARACTER: No, please! You said there'd be no violence!

AUTHOR: It'll be painless.

CHARACTER: You bastard!

AUTHOR: (*Solemnly putting pen to paper*) And sadly, after many months of struggle, our tragic orphan's vital organs began to fail.

CHARACTER: No, please!

AUTHOR: It all happened so suddenly – so unexpectedly. There was nothing anyone could do. The doctor turned his head away in resignation.

CHARACTER: Please, no!

AUTHOR: The author looked toward the heavens in search of solace…and perhaps…a little inspiration.

CHARACTER: Please, I beg of you!

AUTHOR: Unable to fight any longer, the poor wretch finally breathed its last breath.

> (*CHARACTER breaths heavily, then slumps forward onto the table. Pause.*)

AUTHOR: And then…the poor devil was gone. Such a short, sad life, truncated – perhaps mercifully – by a ruthless disease and a writer's frustration. (*Beat*) The end.

> (*AUTHOR tears out a page from the pad, screws it into a ball and throws it across the room.*)

AUTHOR: Now what?

> (*As the AUTHOR buries his head in his hands, the lights fade down to BLACK.*)

END OF PLAY

THE SKEWED PICTURE

THE SKEWED PICTURE

CHARACTERS

BETTY: An avid cruciverbalist.

BOB: An avid reader.

SETTING & TIME

SETTING: A living room.

TIME: The present.

At rise: BETTY *and* BOB *are discovered sitting on a sofa, downstage C.* BETTY *is studiously working on a crossword puzzle, while* BOB *is completely engrossed in a book that he's reading. After several moments,* BOB *suddenly and quite dramatically slams the book shut, causing* BETTY *to jump.*

BETTY: Oh!

BOB: That is absolutely, positively, undeniably the most astonishing thing that I have ever read in my entire life – ever!

BETTY: Yes, well…do you think you could do it a bit more quietly, please?

BOB: Astounding!

BETTY: (*Refocused back on her puzzle*) Mmm…

BOB: Earth shattering!

BETTY: That's nice.

BOB: It's almost...too much to get my head around.

BETTY: So's twenty-two across. (*Beat*) What's an eight-letter word for "memory meltdown"?

BOB: This changes everything, Betty. Everything we ever thought we knew and understood about our existence has just been turned on its head and tossed out the window – it's that big!

BETTY: It's frustrating is what it is. Fancy having your memory fail you on a clue called "memory meltdown."

BOB: But Betty...don't you want to know my discovery?

BETTY: Oh. Oh, yes of course. (*Putting down her puzzle*) What is it, then?

BOB: Betty...are you familiar with...a parallel universe?

BETTY: It's popped up from time to time, yes.

BOB: It has?

BETTY: Yes. Every now and then.

BOB: (*Cautiously scanning the room*) Where, exactly?

BETTY: In the crossword.

BOB: Oh. No, no, no. Betty, what I'm asking is, are you able to fully comprehend what the existence of a parallel universe would actually mean in the true metaphysical sense?

BETTY: Um...I can't honestly say yes to that...so no.

BOB: No...no, because it's almost unthinkable, isn't it?

BETTY: Yes, I suppose so.

BOB: The implications of it are mind-blowing...frightening, even.

BETTY: What is it, then?

BOB: What it is, Betty...is a separate, entirely self-contained universe that coexists on the same parallel as our very own. Coexists, Betty. Just think about that.

BETTY: Another universe...right here?

BOB: Yes.

BETTY: In our living room?

BOB: Quite possibly.

BETTY: It must be quite a small one, then. Where is it, do you think?

BOB: Aha! That's the mystery. That's what we don't know.

BETTY: So how do you know it's there?

BOB: Oh, it's there all right. There's been all manner of research and studies done on this. Countless studies. It's undeniable. Irrefutable.

BETTY: But how did it get there?

BOB: Well, I, uh…as I understand it, it was, um…the result of a, uh…a quantum event.

BETTY: Which is what?

BOB: That, I'm, um…not *entirely* sure of, but I do have it on good authority.

BETTY: Oh.

BOB: Remarkable, isn't it? When I sat down here on this couch with you not thirty minutes ago, I thought it was just the two of us settling down to exercise our grey matter for a while. Little did *I* know.

BETTY: I still don't know.

BOB: Betty, it's all changed, don't you see?

BETTY: What's changed?

BOB: *Everything.*

BETTY: (*Cautiously scanning the room*) It all looks the same to me.

BOB: Ah, yes, it may look the same to the naked eye, but that doesn't mean that it is the same.

BETTY: Doesn't it?

BOB: Not at all – because now we know, don't we?

BETTY: Um…yes.

BOB: Now we're aware of that parallel universe. Here we are, Betty…sitting here, coexisting with it. Isn't it incredible?

BETTY: Mmm.

BOB: I wonder where it is, exactly. (*Beat*) Perhaps it's right here… (*Gesturing towards the fourth wall*) Right in front of our very eyes.

BETTY: But that's our wall.

BOB: Yes, yes, it may look like our wall to you and me…

>   (BOB *gets up from the sofa and places his hands flat against the fourth wall.*)

BOB: It may even feel like our wall…but perhaps it isn't our wall. Perhaps it's…a quantum event.

BETTY: Well, if it is a quantum event it's got our picture hanging on it.

BOB: Yes, and a little askew, if I'm not mistaken.

>   (BOB *makes a small adjustment to the picture that hangs on the fourth wall.*)

BETTY: Are you sure about all this, Bob?

BOB: Never more certain.

BETTY: Because I just see a wall.

BOB: Yes, we both see a wall. It's what we're meant to see. But if in fact, as I'm becoming increasingly convinced, this is not really a wall at all but a quantum event, then what we see before us could actually function as some sort of inter-universe two-way mirror.

BETTY: Oh.

BOB: Just imagine…right now, right as we speak, there could be someone – hell, there could be a whole room full of people – just sitting there, staring at us.

BETTY: Why would they want to do that?

BOB: I've no idea.

> (BETTY *gets up from the sofa and stands next to BOB, staring at the* *fourth wall.*)

BETTY: Perhaps they're lonely?

BOB: Oh, I don't think so. I expect they're just curious.

BETTY: About us?

BOB: Yes.

BETTY: I don't know why…I wouldn't be.

BOB: Perhaps in observing us – in studying us – they're hoping to see something of themselves in us, and consequently find a sort of catharsis in our shared experience. I think they're hoping to learn things from us that they can take away and apply to their own lives in their own universe.

BETTY: I don't think they'll learn very much watching you read a book and me do the crossword.

BOB: Well, perhaps not at this precise juncture, but, um…well, at other times…when we're more animated and, um…well, busy being us.

BETTY: Just a minute! You don't suppose this two-way mirror thing extends all the way to our bedroom and bathroom, do you? I wouldn't want them looking at us when we're…you know…exposed.

BOB: Oh my goodness, no. I don't imagine for a second that a quantum event would ever be caught dabbling in smut.

BETTY: Thank heavens. Gave me a bit of a turn just thinking of it.

BOB: No, I'm sure it's all aboveboard and confined only to this room. If there is anyone out there looking at us, I'm sure they have absolutely no interest in probing our more sensitive areas.

(*Pause.*)

BETTY: I wonder if they're forced to do it.

BOB: To come and look at us?

BETTY: Yes.

BOB: Oh, I wouldn't think so. (*Beat*) One or two of them, perhaps.

BETTY: They could be. They could live in some sort of totalitarian state where they're forced into rooms and made to look at ordinary people going about their business, no matter how boring it gets. Perhaps it's a form of torture?

BOB: Oh dear me, Betty, you *are* putting a bleak spin on things, aren't you? (*Beat*) No, I prefer to think of it as something…cultural.

BETTY: Cultural? Us?

BOB: Well…not *us* necessarily – although I do believe my choice of reading material does denote the hallmarks of an enlightened mind – but in general, yes, I wouldn't be surprised if many of them are gazing at us in search of some form of…edification.

BETTY: That pops up now and then, too.

BOB: What does?

BETTY: Edification…in the crossword.

BOB: Ah.

BETTY: I always think it has something to do with eating, for some reason. (*Beat*) I wonder what they look like.

BOB: Just like us, I expect.

BETTY: What do you mean, like…clones?

BOB: No, no, just regular people…all types, all stripes.

BETTY: Mmm… (*Beat*) It's a bit eerie if you think about it, isn't it? I mean, even though it still looks like our wall, if I think about it long enough…well, I can almost feel them looking at me right now…feel their eyes all over me.

BOB: Steady on, Betty. No need for hysterics.

(*Pause.*)

BETTY: Here's a thought.

34

BOB: Hmm?

BETTY: Perhaps they're just looking to be entertained.

BOB: Oh, no! Oh my goodness me, no! No, no, no, no, no! This is...really, I'm...I am very disappointed in you, Betty... *very* disappointed.

BETTY: Well, they might.

BOB: How could you even contemplate such a thought? Here we are, knee-deep in quantum events and the warping of space and time, and somehow you see fit to reduce everything down to the level of the boulevard. I find this *most* disturbing and *highly* inappropriate.

BETTY: It was just a thought.

BOB: They're probably all sophisticates and aesthetes with a hankering for the lofty. They wouldn't be looking for cheap entertainment or silly distractions. These poor people are probably *desperate* for some sort of meaningful cultural experience – I can almost feel it oozing from them. They're starved and they're looking to us for nourishment. And damn it, Betty, we're going to do everything within our power to make sure they get it.

BETTY: We are?

BOB: Yes, we are. We're going to give them all of the culture they'd ever dreamed of and more besides. We'll read the classics to them, every one of them; we'll recite poetry from Keats to Cummings; we'll play them Brahms and Beethoven; we'll reenact every play ever written in any language.

BETTY: Oh.

BOB: We'll sing operas to them; we'll show them our dance steps; we'll read them every thought of every philosopher that ever existed; we'll give them lectures in art history and seminars on mime. By God, Betty, by the time we're done with them, they'll be on their knees, *begging* for a way to thank us!

BETTY: Oh dear!

BOB: Right then, let's get to work. I say we start with some James Joyce. Now where did I put my copy of Finnegan's Wake?

BETTY: Um...

BOB: Did I leave it in the...no, no, not there. Perhaps I put it in the...no, I wouldn't have done that. Did I put it on top of the...but why on earth would I have put it there? Oh, this is all terribly frustrating! (*Beat*) Wait a second...I've just realized something.

BETTY: Oh?

BOB: Your crossword puzzle.

BETTY: Yes?

BOB: Twenty-two across...an eight-letter word for "memory meltdown."

BETTY: What?

BOB: Isn't it obvious?

BETTY: Is it?

BOB: Blackout!

BETTY: (*With great relief*) Blackout!

(*BLACKOUT.*)

END OF PLAY

FILLER

FILLER

CHARACTERS

SHANE: Tries to convey a macho image, but in truth is nervous and vulnerable. Perhaps a slight Cockney accent. 20s/30s.

TATYANA: Pragmatic, level-headed, but not without heart. Perhaps a slight Eastern European accent. 20s/30s.

SETTING & TIME

SETTING: An ominous and dimly lit stage.

TIME: The present.

At rise: The room is dimly lit. SHANE is seated in a chair, downstage C, holding his head in his hands. TATYANA paces back and forth, upstage. After a while, she stops and appears to peer out of a window, as if looking for something or someone. SHANE turns and observes her.

SHANE: Any sign?

(*Pause.*)

TATYANA: Nothing.

SHANE: (*Rubbing his face in his hands*) Where the fuck is he?

(*Pause.*)

TATYANA: I'm beginning to wonder if they haven't–

SHANE: Shut up! Don't! Don't even think it. We can't afford to.

TATYANA: He was careless. He was stupid. They could have easily–

SHANE: I said, shut it!

(*SHANE covers his face with his face hands again.*)

TATYANA: Yes, yes, bury your head in your hands – in the sand. But when you pull them away, the reality will still be there…waiting for you….for us both.

SHANE: I just need to think, that's all.

TATYANA: About what?

SHANE: About what we do…if he doesn't show up.

TATYANA: What's there to think about? If he doesn't show up…we're dead.

SHANE: *No!*

(*SHANE leaps from his chair and crosses to TATYANA, grabbing her roughly by the shoulders.*)

SHANE: Listen to me, Tatyana, and listen good! He'll be here. I know he will. Something's happened. Something's screwed up his timing. But he'll be here. I know it. (*Beat*) And if he isn't…if he's…then we'll…change plans.

TATYANA: To what? There are no others. It all depends on him.

42

SHANE: No it doesn't! We still have options. (*Beat*) I just...

(*SHANE returns to the chair and rubs his head in hands once more.*)

TATYANA: Look, this is a one-way street. You knew the risks when you got into this. If you don't have the guts to follow through when things go wrong, then you should never have got involved to begin with. This operation can't afford people like you.

SHANE: Hey, it's not my fault he hasn't shown up. It's no good blaming me.

TATYANA: No one's blaming anyone. But if you can't keep your head in a crisis you shouldn't be in this business.

SHANE: It's keeping my head I'm concerned about. Now, instead of just standing there criticizing, why don't you try and help figure out how we're gonna get out of this mess if he doesn't show up.

TATYANA: He's not showing up.

SHANE: A real optimist, you are, aren't you?

(*Pause.*)

TATYANA: I think I've figured it out.

SHANE: Figured what out?

TATYANA: This. Us. All of this...perpetual waiting.

SHANE: What's to figure out? We're waiting for him to show up, that's all.

TATYANA: But I told you…he's not showing up.

SHANE: Not yet.

TATYANA: He's not showing up because he was never intended to show up. (*Beat*) It's all a set up.

(*Pause.*)

SHANE: What are you talking about?

TATYANA: Us. This. We've been set up.

SHANE: By…by who?

TATYANA: I'll give you one guess.

(*Pause.*)

SHANE: I don't…I've no idea.

(*Pause.*)

TATYANA: The playwright.

SHANE: (*Incredulous*) *What?*

TATYANA: You heard me.

SHANE: But…that's insane.

TATYANA: Is it? Think about it. Think about how neatly the last scene was resolved – how the scene following this one starts from an entirely different plot point.

SHANE: That doesn't mean anything.

TATYANA: No? Then why are we never mentioned again for the rest of the play?

SHANE: That's not true. We are. We are mentioned.

TATYANA: Near the end in a brief aside from a minor character to tie up a loose thread, that's all. The quick disposal of a thin subplot that was never intended to go anywhere in the first place.

SHANE: No...no, you've got it all wrong.

TATYANA: Shane, listen to me, this scene is completely unnecessary to the overall arc of the story. You know it and I know it. It neither propels the play forward nor adds anything of value to the central plot.

SHANE: And you...you really believe this?

TATYANA: I've had my suspicions for some time, but tonight...tonight the final pieces of the puzzle fell into place. You see, I'd often wondered why our characters were brought back from scene three in such a seemingly random and superfluous way. And tonight it hit me.

SHANE: What did?

TATYANA: This entire scene – this completely meaningless waiting game – was added after he'd completed the original script.

SHANE: No!

TATYANA: I'm guessing somewhere around the third or fourth

draft.

SHANE: But why? Why on earth would he do that?

TATYANA: Isn't it obvious? It wasn't long enough. He doubtless foresaw problems getting it produced if it didn't stretch to a full evening's entertainment, so he decided to…pad it out.

SHANE: Oh my God! That means…that means that we're…

TATYANA: Yes, Shane. It's time we faced the truth. And the truth is that you and I are little more than…filler.

SHANE: No! (*He begins pacing the stage, highly agitated.*) Jesus Christ, we've gotta do something! We can't just continue on like this!

TATYANA: Do what? We're merely pawns in this web of deceit. We have no say in it.

SHANE: But we have to do *something*. This is ridiculous. We'll be a laughing stock.

TATYANA: I fear it may already be too late.

SHANE: So…what happens now?

TATYANA: What always happens…we wait.

SHANE: I don't know that I can. Not now. Not now that I know.

TATYANA: What choice do you have?

SHANE: But to stay here and just wait – knowing it's all pointless? Knowing we're just killing time because of a poorly structured play?

TATYANA: We've done it countless times before and we'll do it again.

SHANE: But that was before we knew. Oh God, this is…this is torture.

TATYANA: I doubt it's a walk in the park for the audience, either. Let's hope they remain intrigued enough by the mystery of who we're waiting for and don't start putting two and two together.

SHANE: This is unconscionable. How could he get away with it?

TATYANA: It doesn't matter how, the fact is he has. Anyway, it's nothing new – I see it all the time.

SHANE: I should have guessed. Why didn't I see it?

TATYANA: Don't blame yourself.

SHANE: I should have realized the whole concept was suspect. Two people just sitting around waiting for someone who never shows up – I mean, who could possibly find that interesting?

TATYANA: (*Shrugs*) People are strange. Perhaps they read more into it – see it as some sort of…I don't know…metaphor.

SHANE: Well, I don't. I see it as a cheap cop-out from a lazy writer bankrupt of both ideas and principles.

(*Pause.*)

TATYANA: And yet still we wait.

SHANE: Not me. Not for much longer.

TATYANA: You have no choice, Shane. What's written is written. There's nothing to be done.

SHANE: But I...I can't be a party to this. It's a...a waste of people's time.

TATYANA: Relax. They waste much more of it in far more trivial ways. At least with us they have a semi-respectable excuse.

SHANE: Which is what?

TATYANA: "I went to see a play."

(*Pause.*)

SHANE: So we just...wait...until the end?

TATYANA: Yes, Shane. I'm afraid so.

(*Pause.*)

SHANE: Oh, no!

TATYANA: What?

SHANE: Oh, shit!

TATYANA: What is it?

SHANE: I can't...I can't think straight, it's all...all this crap about the playwright and the scene, it's...it's fucked with my head. I don't... (*Beat*) I don't remember.

TATYANA: Don't remember what?

48

SHANE: How it ends.

TATYANA: Our scene?

SHANE: Yes.

TATYANA: It's nothing to worry about. It ends very simply. (*Beat*) It ends when the light goes out.

SHANE: That's it?

TATYANA: Yes.

SHANE: All that waiting…all that hoping…and it all just ends…just like that?

TATYANA: Yes.

SHANE: So it was all…pointless?

TATYANA: Well…that depends on how you look at it.

SHANE: But we had all that hope – all that expectation. And then it just ends. Unfulfilled.

TATYANA: Not unfulfilled. Unanswered.

SHANE: Isn't that the same thing?

TATYANA: No. One is a dead end. The other is a question mark.

SHANE: You mean a mystery?

TATYANA: In a way.

SHANE: So it…it was all worth, then? Our scene did mean something after all?

TATYANA: In the grand scheme of the play, probably not. We have our turn in the spotlight, eventually the light goes out, and in truth, we're mentioned again but not really remembered.

SHANE: So…so we really are just…filler?

TATYANA: I wouldn't say that. (*Beat*) Now that I look at it, it's really not been that bad. We had our time together, you and me, and on the whole you were pretty good company to share it with. (*Beat*) And anyway, it couldn't go on forever.

SHANE: No.

TATYANA: So, all in all, I'd say it was worth it.

SHANE: Yeah…yeah, I think so, too.

TATYANA: Good. Now give me your hand.

SHANE: Why? This isn't a…does it become a love scene?

TATYANA: No, Shane, mercifully not. But it is the end.

SHANE: It is?

TATYANA: Yes.

SHANE: Are you sure?

TATYANA: My memory's better than yours, remember?

SHANE: Oh, yeah. I'd forgotten.

(*SHANE places his hand in TATYANA'S.*)

TATYANA: Are you ready?

SHANE: For what?

TATYANA: For what comes next.

SHANE: And what's that?

TATYANA: Ah…well, I'm afraid even I don't know the answer to that.

SHANE: Oh. (*Beat*) That's okay.

TATYANA: Trust me?

SHANE: Yes.

(*Pause.*)

TATYANA: Very well, then…our moment's up. Time to go.

(*They both look skyward as the lights slowly fade down to BLACK.*)

END OF PLAY

THE CURIOUS ART OF CRITIQUE

THE CURIOUS ART OF CRITIQUE

CHARACTERS

ART: The Director. Age open.

JAMES: Receiving notes from the director. 20s/30s.

STEPHANIE: Receiving notes from the director. 20s/30s.

SETTING & TIME

SETTING: A stage.

TIME: The present.

At rise: There is a table downstage C. with three chairs placed around it. In the stage R. chair sits JAMES, and in the stage L. chair sits ART. The chair between them is empty. ART is holding his head in his hands. After a moment he looks up and sighs heavily.

ART: The thing is, Jim…oh, may I call you Jim? I know it's James, but I like to feel that we're… (*Gesturing with his hands to make his point*) Do you know what I mean?

JAMES: Yeah, yeah.

ART: It just makes it more…I don't know…*real.*

JAMES: Sure.

ART: Especially in a little one-on-one like this.

JAMES: Yeah, no problem.

ART: I'm so glad. I'm Arthur, of course, but…to you, Jim…I am *Art.*

JAMES: Yeah, all right, Art – so what's the problem?

ART: Don't you just hate that word…*problem?*

JAMES: No, not really.

ART: No? Oh, I do – *loathe* it. Anyway…the reason I wanted to have this little chat with you, Jim, is because…well, first off, let me say this has absolutely nothing to do with your performance this evening.

JAMES: Okay.

ART: Nothing. Zero. Zip.

JAMES: Well…that's good.

ART: Because what you have to offer is nothing short of…sensational.

JAMES: Really?

ART: Oh, yes. I would describe you as a *major* talent.

JAMES: *Really?*

ART: Quite remarkable.

JAMES: Wow!

ART: Don't sound so surprised. Surely you're aware of the extraordinary gifts you possess?

JAMES: Well, I…you know…I suppose we all like to think we have…*something*.

ART: I'm more inclined to think that you, Jim, have everything…and more besides.

JAMES: Whoa! That's amazing. Can you really tell…I mean…just from what you've seen tonight?

ART: I have been in this business for *many* years, Jim. Many, many years. I've seen it all. But rarely do I ever come across…whatever it is that you have.

JAMES: I'm…I don't know what to say. I'm humbled.

ART: Be humbled, Jim. But not by my words – by your own brilliance.

JAMES: And you could see all that…here tonight.

ART: Oh, yes. I was watching you *very* carefully. *You* specifically.

JAMES: Wow. Good job I didn't know or I'd have probably been, you know…thrown off.

ART: Yes. Which rather brings me to the main reason for this little tête-à-tête.

JAMES: Okay.

ART: You see, it would be remiss of me, regardless of your bountiful talents, if I didn't point out... (*Sighs heavily*) Oh, how do I put this without sounding harsh? (*Beat*) Areas for improvement?

JAMES: Well, yeah, of course. I mean, you're the director.

ART: Yes. Yes, I am, Jim. The success or failure of the entire production rests on my shoulders alone. It is an *immense* responsibility that would *crush* a lesser man. And I do not take it lightly. And for that reason alone, I am forced to return to that most vile of all words...*problem*.

JAMES: Well, if it's not right, you know...you gotta let me know.

ART: Yes. Yes, I must. (*Suddenly stands and clasps his head in his hands*) God, I hate my job sometimes!

JAMES: No, no, it's okay, really. I...I don't mind.

ART: But *I* mind, Jim. *I* mind. It all just seems so ridiculous somehow, don't you think? All this finding fault and criticizing, when all you really want to do is enjoy everything your eyes are bearing witness to...to be swept away in its rapture.

JAMES: Not if there's a fault, no.

ART: Oh, this mad, insane profession! *Why* did I allow it to seduce me?

JAMES: I expect...because you love it, Art.

(*ART sits back down in his chair and regains his composure.*)

ART: Yes. (*Beat*) Yes, I suspect you're right, Jim. It may have taken

58

me by force, but…ever since, I've been smitten – prostrate and yielding to its every whim.

JAMES: Yeah, well, so um…what's the problem?

ART: Ah, yes, the, um…*problem*. Yes, well…uh…perhaps this would be a good time to bring in Stephanie.

JAMES: Stephanie?

ART: Yes. You don't mind, do you?

JAMES: Uh…no, no.

ART: (*Calling off*) Stephanie! Stephanie, dear! I'm ready for you now!

(*STEPHANIE enters from stage R. looking nervous and confused.*)

ART: There she is! What an angel – and pretty as a picture. Sit down here, my love, next to me.

(*STEPHANIE sits in the empty chair between ART and JAMES. STEPHANIE and JAMES nod and smile at each other.*)

ART: Stephanie, can I first tell you that you were *magnificent* out there tonight. Dare I use the word…dynamite?

STEPHANIE: Oh…well, thank you. Thanks very much.

ART: I had my eye on you, too, you see? Eyes like a hawk, even with contacts.

STEPHANIE: Well, it's…nice to be noticed…amongst all the rest.

ART: Steph, Steph, who could *not* notice you? You were like a beacon out there. Sailors could sail their ships by that luminous face alone.

STEPHANIE: Ohh…what a lovely thing to say.

ART: What a lovely gift to have.

STEPHANIE: Well, I…I do my best.

ART: Yes. I know you do. (*Tentatively*) But…

STEPHANIE: But?

ART: Well…oh, this is so difficult. Sometimes, as I was telling young Jim here…sometimes your "best" needs… (*Wincing*) A little more.

STEPHANIE: More?

JAMES: You want more?

ART: (*Affecting a cringing expression*) Hate me. Hate me now, please. Get it over with.

STEPHANIE: I don't hate you.

JAMES: No, I don't either. Just tell us what you want us to do.

ART: May I? May I really?

JAMES: Of course.

STEPHANIE: Yeah, don't be silly, just let me know.

ART: Oh, bless you both. However did I end up with two such big-hearted, powerhouse superstars in my theatre? (*In an abrupt change of tone*) Right, Jim, let's start with you.

JAMES: Okay.

ART: This play…it contains humor. Not a lot, I admit. But it's there. And with you…I'm just not seeing it.

JAMES: Well, there's some lines here and there, I suppose, but on the whole it's a bit of a downer.

ART: Yes, yes, but that's because it's what we call a *tra-gi-com-edy*. It's *Chekhovian*. It's where we find the humor amidst the pain. It helps us get through it. It's cathartic. And I don't see the pleasure…in the pain…so I need more pleasure.

JAMES: All right, but—

ART: Smile for me.

JAMES: What?

ART: Give me a smile. The best you've got.

(*JAMES smiles awkwardly.*)

ART: (*Covering his eyes and turning away*) Urgh!

JAMES: It's…well, it's not easy to smile when someone just asks you to. You need a…a reason.

ART: I don't. Never have. But that's beside the point. You, Jim, must *think* of something funny. Dig within yourself. What do you kids

61

laugh at today? Amputees? Poor people? Midgets? Whatever it is, you must *find* the answer within yourself.

JAMES: Uh…um…oh, I don't know. You need to hear a joke to laugh. And there aren't any in this play.

ART: Not jokes, Jim, but *humor*.

JAMES: But…can't you just *think* something's funny? Think it but not show it?

ART: Oh, no, Jim. I need to see a response to the material. I need to know – *to see* – that the meaning of the author's work is hitting its mark. That's my job.

JAMES: All right, well, I'll…I'll try harder to show it. Smile and laugh more…if that's what you want.

ART: It is, Jim – in the right places. And I thank you…from the *bottom* of my showbiz-loving heart.

JAMES: I'll do my best.

ART: You're a star. (In another abrupt change of tone) Stephanie!

(*STEPHANIE jumps, startled by the sudden and brusque shift of tone and attention.*)

STEPHANIE: Yes!

ART: (*Sighs*) Oh, Stephanie. Steph, Steph, Steph. Just look at you. Who could possibly find fault with you?

STEPHANIE: (*With a bashful giggle*) Oh!

ART: Except me. (*Beat*) You see, the problem is, Steph – and it's a big one – is that this play, despite its moments of levity, is in essence a work of *soul-destroying* tragedy. At its core, it is bleak, desolate, and utterly inconsolable. It has an ugly heart of darkness that is at once an indictment of the human condition and a testament to it. *That* is what I want it to show. *That* is what I want people to feel. Are you with me?

STEPHANIE: Yes.

ART: So why do you give me *nothing?*

STEPHANIE: Nothing?

ART: *Nothing.* When I look at you, it's as if I were watching CSPAN.

STEPHANIE: But, I-I–

ART: Trust me, Steph, *believe* me, I can tell what a truly loving, feeling, caring person you are deep down inside.

STEPHANIE: Oh, I am, I am!

ART: But all I'm seeing is an ice queen.

STEPHANIE: (*Shocked*) A what?

ART: You heard right. *But...*don't despair...well, do despair, that's the point...*but*, I think I may have a solution for you. I'm sure you're very familiar with the teachings of Constantin Stanislavski.

STEPHANIE: Um–

ART: And of his 'system' and most especially of his introduction of the use of 'emotion memory.' And *that* is what I want from you, Steph. I want you to *feel* the raw pain of what's happening on stage by internally reliving some unspeakable, painful, catastrophic event that occurred in your own life. So, come on – what do you have?

STEPHANIE: Well, I don't know that I want to…I mean…it's a bit personal, really. Don't you think?

ART: *Art…* is personal. There is nothing *more* personal. Now, come along, stop being so coy and precious and tell me something truly, truly horrible that you lived through. We all have one. And I want horrid with a big 'H.'

STEPHANIE: I'm…I'm thinking.

ART: Dig deep, Stephanie. I want real human misery. So what is it? There has to be something. Something that scarred you like nothing else. Something that shut your world down. Something that still tortures you to this very day. The love of your life that dumped you for your best friend? A dearly beloved pet that passed away? A relative gassed in the Holocaust? Anything, something – you have to give me *something*, Stephanie.

STEPHANIE: Well…

ART: Yes?

STEPHANIE: I don't…tell many people about this, but…

ART: Yes, yes?

STEPHANIE: When I was seven-years-old, my mother…committed suicide in front of me. Hanged herself.

ART: (*Ecstatically*) *Yes!*

STEPHANIE: She didn't mean to…in front of me, I mean. I just walked in at the wrong time…just as she was doing it. And there was nothing I could do. I didn't understand what was happening…what I was seeing. It was all weird. I was only seven.

ART: Of course you didn't – of course you were. Oh, this is *pure gold!* Now, just imagine this: Imagine the very last thoughts that were going through her head as she was dangling from that homemade noose, seeing her precious little daughter below her, knowing she'd just emotionally crippled and scarred her for the rest of her life, and there was nothing, absolutely *nothing* she could do about it…it was too late.

STEPHANIE: (*Sobbing*) I know, I know, I think of that.

ART: Such a haunted, tortured death.

STEPHANIE: Yes.

ART: Knowing that her final, grotesque, selfish act would ripple painfully through the life of her simple, innocent young child.

STEPHANIE: (*Crying uncontrollably*) Yes, yes.

ART: Yes, and *that* is what I need to see from you, Stephanie! *That* is emotion! *That* is what I've been searching for. I knew it was there – it just needed someone like me to bring it out.

(*ART stands and beckons the others to do the same.*)

ART: All right, let's get on with the show!

(JAMES and STEPHANIE stand and move downstage, STEPHANIE still sobbing. ART puts his arms around them both and leads them to the edge of the stage.)

ART: I don't deserve either of you, I really don't. Now, you go out there, you take your seats again, and you make me proud! Be the best audience you can be!

(JAMES and STEPHANIE step down from the stage and begin walking up the aisle.)

ART: *(Calling after them)* Enjoy the rest of the show! It's all for you! And remember, *feel* it, *live* it! *(Clenching his fists triumphantly)* I love you guys! *(Clasping his hands to his heart)* Every blessed one of you.

(ART turns his back and spreads his arms, forefingers pointed up and out.)

ART: Okay, everybody – intermission over! Act two places please! Now let's make some *magic!*

(As ART snaps his fingers the lights BLACKOUT.)

END OF PLAY

WHAT'S THE META?

WHAT'S THE META?

CHARACTERS

PART 1: A written part in a script.

PART 2: A written part in a script.

Note: Both parts can be performed by any age, race, gender/orientation, etc. and in any combination thereof.

SETTING & TIME

SETTING: A stage.

TIME: The present.

Two PARTS on a stage in tableaux. After a moment, PART 1 emits a deep sigh. PART 2 turns and looks briefly at PART 1 before returning to their original pose. Soon after, PART 1 elicits another deep sigh.

PART 2: (*Looking back again*) Is something wrong?

(*PART 1 shrugs off the question dismissively.*)

PART 2: I asked you a question.

PART 1: I know.

PART 2: Well? What's the matter?

PART 1: You wouldn't understand. Don't worry about it.

PART 2: All right, first of all you have but the most rudimentary knowledge of who I am – *me* – so to assume that I wouldn't understand is presumptuous to say the least, and more than a little condescending. And secondly, I *have* to worry about it because I'm alone out here with you and a show's about to begin, so if there is a problem I freely and openly admit to harbouring a desire to see it resolved as quickly as possible. Okay?

PART 1: Whatever.

PART 2: (*Enraged.*) What? How dare you – *dare you!* – *you*, as thoughtfully transcribed literature, utter that mindless catchall phrase that is the embodiment of total, unmitigated verbal and mental atrophy.

PART 1: It's not my fault. (*Beat*) I'm a victim of circumstance.

PART 2: What circumstance? What's your problem? Stop whinging and just out with it.

PART 1: I'm…I don't have…I lack motivation.

PART 2: That's it?

PART 1: Yes.

PART 2: So what's the big deal? I don't have it either. Most people don't. We just have to force ourselves. Force ourselves to go on.

PART 1: I can't. There's nothing there.

PART 2: I know it feels that way sometimes, but you just have to buck up and press on.

PART 1: Oh yes, it's all right for you, isn't it?

PART 2: What do you mean?

PART 1: Because you're…fleshed out.

PART 2: No I'm not.

PART 1: Compared to me you are. You're multi-dimensional. I'm just a cipher. A convenient device thrown in by the writer to expound upon a certain point of view.

PART 2: But you're relevant. You have relevancy. You're integral to the story.

PART 1: Only in a narrative sense. I don't really belong.

PART 2: Don't be so self-pitying.

PART 1: I'm not, I'm just being honest.

PART 2: Look, a major and completely unexpected plot point hinges upon your sudden appearance in the proceedings. Without you the play wouldn't be turned on its head at the end of act one, leaving the audience breathless and gasping in anticipation – on a good night, at least.

PART 1: That's very kind of you and I know you mean well, but I'm not so underwritten as to be painfully aware of the fact that I'm just a tool. And I can accept that – I can. But not happily.

PART 2: I think you're being a bit hard on yourself, don't you?

PART 1: (*Defensively*) *I'm* not being hard on myself. It was all I was given.

PART 2: Then make the most of it.

PART 1: Oh, right! Say's you. It's all right for you – it's all downhill for you. You get to reveal a multitude of levels and depths as you continue your ninety-minute journey from point A to point B. Your character's arc gradually draws the audience in and endears you to them in ways that initially they would never have dreamt possible, leaving them satisfied and intrigued. Much to their astonishment, this person that they found themselves initially repulsed by turns out to be a complex, and all too human representation of someone that they can empathise and identify with. As they walk out of the main door into the night air they feel buoyed from a sense of having spent an evening and some hard-earned money in a rewarding and enlightening manner…with you.

PART 2: What's wrong with that?

PART 1: Nothing at all. But it wasn't my journey they were taking, it was yours. I was just a plot point.

PART 2: A vital one.

PART 1: In your story.

PART 2: In *the* story.

PART 1: In *your* story. I am a catalyst – nothing more. I have no depth. I have no raison d'etre. I have no inner life. (*Beat*) And I damned well want one and I don't care who knows it!

PART 2: I think you've already started to give yourself one, don't you, the way you're carrying on?

PART 1: Perhaps. Perhaps it's a start. (*Beat*) But I shouldn't have to fight for it, and that's my point.

PART 2: Why not? Anything in this life worth a damn is worth fighting for.

PART 1: Maybe so, but it's so much harder for me, don't you see, because I...I lack–

PART 2: (*Impatiently*) Motivation – yes, yes, yes, I got that part.

PART 1: There's no need to be so testy. It's not my fault I was underwritten.

PART 2: No, but it's not mine either. I didn't ask to be written as a bigger part. I didn't ask to be more absorbing and relevant to the current state of the human condition. You're behaving as if it were some sort of competition.

PART 1: Oh, "absorbing" are we now?

PART 2: (*Uncomfortably*) Well...I'm speaking theoretically, of course. I mean...that's the writer's intention, it's nothing to do with me. I'm not saying that I'm personally absorbing, I'm just reflecting the viewpoint of–

PART 1: Is this pre-show, by the way?

PART 2: What?

PART 1: This.

PART 2: This? No.

PART 1: Then what is it?

PART 2: It's, uh…it's pre-pre-show.

(*Pause.*)

PART 1: What's that?

PART 2: It's sort of like…Off-Off-Broadway.

PART 1: Meaning?

PART 2: Well, it's not there, but it's not quite there either…so it's sort of almost not quite there.

PART 1: Where's there?

PART 2: Somewhere else.

PART 1: Sounds very ephemeral.

PART 2: Yes it is – and that's the beauty of it. And by the way, you're sounding more dimensional by the minute.

PART 1: Oh, thank you. Against type, I might add.

PART 2: Indeed.

PART 1: Come to think of it, I meant to ask you about that earlier – are we characters?

PART 2: (*Astonished*) Us?

PART 1: Yes.

PART 2: No, no, no, of course not. I'm happy to see you become a little more well-rounded but don't get over-inflated at the same time.

PART 1: Then what are we?

PART 2: Words! We're just words. Well, not *just* words. Words are the most important part. But after all, we mustn't get too far ahead of ourselves – we still only exist on paper.

PART 1: Then why are we here?

PART 2: I'm not here.

PART 1: You're not?

PART 2: Of course not.

PART 1: Am I?

PART 2: No.

PART 1: (*Dispirited*) But I…I thought I was a character. Or at the very least…struggling to become one out of what little I am.

PART 2: No, no, no, there you go again – you have it all wrong.

PART 1: Then what am I?

PART 2: (*Implicitly*) Ink on paper.

  (*Pause.*)

PART 1: That's all?

PART 2: "*That's all?*" You ingrate! Don't you have the slightest conception of what that means? You *are* the conception, you fool! You are the birth. Without you nothing happens. Without you there is no play. Without you there is no novel, no film, no poem, nor any of their bastard relations. You are the seed – the root of it all.

PART 1: (*Ingenuously*) I don't feel like it.

PART 2: Not you in yourself, necessarily, but in what you represent. You are ink on paper. From quill to laser jet printer, you are and always will be the beginning. Others may mould you and shape you according to their will – for better or worse – but you will always be the font, in every sense of the word. It's what you are.

(*Pause.*)

PART 1: Gosh…I'd never thought about it like that. All of a sudden I…I don't feel so sketched out and plot-convenient. Thank you. Thank you very much.

PART 2: I'm glad. And don't thank me – they weren't my words.

(*Pause.*)

PART 1: So what's next?

PART 2: Pre-show.

PART 1: And that is?

PART 2: When the others take over.

PART 1: Take over what?

PART 2: Us.

PART 1: Which, in strict definition, means?

PART 2: Strictly speaking I wouldn't like to say, but which includes – though is by no means limited to…makeup, gargling, vocal exercises, diarrhoea, frantic last minute line readings, focus, pace, sense memory recall, and stumbling around in the dark trying to find your spot, praying to God that you do before the lights come up and expose you as a co-conspirator in the enormous piece of artifice that you are attempting to lay before a potentially skeptical, though willingly complicit public.

PART 1: Good heavens! (*Beat*) I think I'll just sink back into the paper and relax for a while, if it's all the same to you.

PART 2: Trust me, I'm about to do the same thing.

PART 1: (*Awkwardly*) By the way…well…if you don't mind my asking…are you male or female?

PART 2: Didn't you read the play?

PART 1: (*Somewhat embarrassed*) Yes, but…mostly my bits…skipped the rest. It was a quick read.

PART 2: (*Reprovingly*) Then shame on you. As I told you before, big or small we are all part of a whole and our acknowledgement of that is the only way we can function properly – all working together. If you don't have the last little piece you'll never complete the puzzle.

PART 1: Sorry.

PART 2: Anyway, does it matter?

PART 1: What?

PART 2: My gender?

PART 1: Not to me.

PART 2: So why ask?

PART 1: Well…I was just wondering if you fancied going for a drink – with me.

PART 2: Now?

PART 1: Only if you want to. I'm not trying to…no strings…I just…well, I sort of like you…in a way, and…anyway…

PART 2: As a matter of fact, I would love to – I am, quite literally, dying for a drink. Let's leave them to do what they will – good, bad or just plain incomprehensible.

PART 1: And perhaps afterwards I could show you a bit of my subtext I've been working on.

PART 2: Easy tiger, let's not get carried away. One step at a time.

PART 1: Sorry, I wasn't trying to…(*Gesturing*) Anyway, after you.

PART 2: (*Gesturing*) No, no, I insist – after you. (*Beat*) Did you have somewhere in mind?

PART 1: (*Begins exiting*) No, do you?

PART 2: (*Begins exiting*) No, but I know a nice place on 46th and First.

PART 1: (*Upon exiting*) Sounds like a good place to start.

PART 2: (*Upon exiting*) And end.

(*The lights fade to BLACK.*)

END OF PLAY

A REBEL AMONG THE WRETCHED

A REBEL AMONG THE WRETCHED

CHARACTERS

MOTHER: The mother. 50s/60s.

MARGARET: The daughter. 20s/30s.

BILLY: The son. 20s/30s.

SETTING & TIME

SETTING: An impoverished and godforsaken bare stage.

TIME: The present.

At rise: MOTHER is sitting in an armchair, stage C. She appears to be asleep. After a few moments, however, she suddenly raises her head and yells at the top of her voice.

MOTHER: *Margaret!*

    (*Pause.*)

MOTHER: *Margaret!*

    (*Pause.*)

MOTHER: *Marrr-greeeet!*

(*MARGARET enters hurriedly from stage R.*)

MARGARET: Yes, Mother, what is it?

MOTHER: What the hell took ya so damn long?

MARGARET: I'm...I'm sorry, Mother. I came as quick as I could. I was washing ya bed sheets downstairs.

MOTHER: *Bed* sheets? What d'ya mean *bed* sheets? What other kinda sheets are there, idiot?

MARGARET: Well, I...anyway...it's hard to hear with all the noise of the machines an' the water an' what-not.

MOTHER: Stop ya blatherin' girl. I don't wanna hear ya problems or excuses – they're always the same.

MARGARET: But it's the truth, Mother. Them machines are old an' they make such a noise ya can hardly hear yourself think.

MOTHER: Well, I can't see as how that would cause ya too much of an inconvenience. Not like there's much goin' on up there to begin with, is there?

MARGARET: (*Defensively*) Yes. Yes, there is, Mother. I've a good mind, I know I do. I just...never had the opportunity, that's all.

MOTHER: For what?

MARGARET: An education. A proper education. Ever since ya problems started, I've had to–

MOTHER: Oh, so now I'm the reason ya stupid?

MARGARET: No, it's not…I'm not saying that, of course not. It's just…if I'd had the chance, I think I could've…well…I think I could've done quite well.

MOTHER: Ya got no skills, girl – 'cept lookin after me – an the sooner off ya realize that, the better off we'll all be.

MARGARET: I know I'm not stupid, Mother. I know I'm not. I don't have no certificates or fancy embossed papers sayin otherwise, but I know I'm not stupid.

MOTHER: Well…as long as you believe it, honey, I guess that's all that matters. Now, if ya wouldn't mind switchin them thoughts in that tiny little mind o' yours to start thinkin 'bout me for just a second or two here, I'd greatly appreciate it. (*Beat*) For Christ's sake, I'm the one dyin here!

MARGARET: I'm sorry, Mother. I-I got a bit carried away, I guess. What is it ya need? Is it a drink? Ya want me to fix ya another drink?

MOTHER: *No! No*, I don't want another damn drink! Is that what you want? Ya wanna poison ma liver an' keep pushin me a little closer to the grave? Is that it?

MARGARET: No, Mother, I–

MOTHER: When I wanna 'nother damn drink you'll damn well know it!

MARGARET: Of course, Mother. (*Beat*) Is it ya pills, maybe? Can I fetch ya pills for ya?

MOTHER: Oh yeah, you'd just love that, wouldn't ya? Fetch Mama some more pills so ya can knock her out for another couple of hours. (*Beat*) Well, guess what? It ain't gonna happen this time, sweetheart.

MARGARET: Mother, all I was trying to do was–

MOTHER: *Don't* tell me what you was tryin to do! I know all your little schemin' ways an' tricks, an' don't ever think I don't. (*Beat*) Thing of it is, though…none of it matters no more. (*Beat*) 'Cause I want out.

MARGARET: Out?

MOTHER: You heard right, missy – *out!*

MARGARET: You…ya wanna go outside for a bit? Ya wanna get some air? (*Gesturing to help her*) If ya grab your stick an' put your arm 'round ma shoulders, I'm sure maybe we can–

MOTHER: Get away from me, girl!

MARGARET: But I…I thought ya–

MOTHER: I don't mean outta this *house!* I mean outta this god-damned, lousy, miserable *play!*

MARGARET: (*Aghast*) Mother! How…how can you say such a thing?

MOTHER: 'Cause I gotta mouth an' I can make it say stuff, that's how. An' I've had it! I'm up to here with it. An' I want out!

MARGARET: You don't mean this, Mother, I know ya don't. You're just tired is all.

MOTHER: Ya got that right – tired o' this miserable, stinkin family. Tired of all its damn problems. Tired of sittin in this chair night after night spittin ma bile an' bitterness at anyone in sight.

MARGARET: But…but ya can't just up an' leave, Mother. You're the center of the family. What on earth would we all do with you gone?

MOTHER: Well, I guess you an' all the rest o' this sorry, messed up clan are gonna have to start figurin stuff out for yourselves, aren't ya?

MARGARET: I-I just don't understand. What's brought all this on so sudden?

MOTHER: Ain't nothin sudden about it. Been a *long* time comin. I guess I just reached that point where enough's enough.

MARGARET: Are ya…are ya not happy here, Mother?

MOTHER: Well, now…why don't ya just reflect a while on that there question ya just posed to me, young Margaret, an' I've a feelin you'll have your answer in no time at all…bein so smart an' all.

MARGARET: I know it ain't all fun an' games, but we–

MOTHER: No, it ain't! It's nothin but a bunch of unfulfilled lives simmerin with resentment, day in an' day out. An' that's what I want – out!

MARGARET: But why now?

MOTHER: While I still got some life in me, that's why now. I'm old, alcoholic, addicted to prescription drugs, an' this soul-destroyin, downer of a play's suckin the life outta me!

MARGARET: But where would ya go? What would ya do?

MOTHER: I'll find my self somethin better, that's what. A musical, maybe. Somethin where everyone's singin an' dancing an' havin a good time of it.

MARGARET: A…a musical? But that's fluff, Mother. It ain't nothin. Why would ya wanna be in somethin like that?

MOTHER: So I could enjoy myself, stupid. So I wouldn't have to sit around here starin at your long, loveless face six nights a week, plus matinees.

MARGARET: But surely you're too…

MOTHER: Too what? *Old?*

MARGARET: Well, ya ain't exactly–

MOTHER: Don't you worry that tiny little mind o' yours about that, my girl. Still plenty of old croaks out there makin the rounds.

> (*Just at that moment, BILLY enters from stage L. MARGARET gasps in shock.*)

MARGARET: Billy!

BILLY: Hello, Margaret.

MARGARET: What on earth? Ya…ya came back!

BILLY: Yes, I did. It's been a long time.

MOTHER: Well, well…if it ain't the prodigal son makin his return to the family rats nest…right on cue.

BILLY: It's very nice to see you, too, Mother.

MOTHER: Let me guess. Ya been livin in some fancy city somewhere, workin an' strugglin' ya way up until ya finally made somethin of yourself. Only trouble is, ya still can't get the dirt out from between ya toes, nor the poison in the pit of ya soul, so ya came back here to try an' get it all cleaned up. Close?

BILLY: I may have changed in some ways, Mother, but clearly you haven't. You're exactly the same.

MOTHER: Not for long.

MARGARET: Billy, oh, Billy! Ya come back just in time. Somethin awful's goin down.

BILLY: What?

MARGARET: It's Mother – she's leavin.

BILLY: Leaving?

MARGARET: She wants outta the play!

BILLY: Mother! Mother, you can't do that.

MOTHER: Who the hell are you to tell me what I can and can't do? Ya come waltzin' in here after all these years in ya fancy clothes, with ya fancy manners, thinkin you're somethin better than the rest of us. Well, ya ain't! Ya trash. Ya always were an' ya always will be. Trash in a fancy suit's still trash, an' I'm done with the lot o' ya!

89

BILLY: But…but you can't. You mustn't. I have a whole host of unresolved problems to work through before the end of the play.

MOTHER: Too bad.

BILLY: But…but what about my issues?

MOTHER: Stick em up ya–

MARGARET: Mother! (*Beat*) Mother, would ya please just think again? Think about what you'd be doin to the family – to a respected work of drama.

MOTHER: I'm done thinkin. I'm goin.

BILLY: But you've got nowhere to go.

MARGARET: She's talkin 'bout joinin a musical.

BILLY: You're not serious?

MARGARET: Says she wants to sing an' dance.

BILLY: Margaret, we have to do something – call someone. This is far more serious than I thought.

MOTHER: What's wrong with a goddamned musical? Don't you people ever smile, for Christ's sake?

BILLY: Mother, it's cheap, frivolous nonsense. It's lowbrow spectacle that panders shamelessly to the masses. *This* is a multi-award winning family drama that's been translated into seventeen languages and was hailed by the New York Times as "Harrowing, ground-breaking, and absolutely unmissable." Stars still line up to play the leads, and it's been on every critic's "best of" list since its debut. Why would you give all of that up for some silly, clichéd, theatrical by-product?

MOTHER: Because it's *fun*, ya lifeless duds! Because it ain't some big, ugly, self-pityin, slice o' shitty life. By God, it was a humorless day I shat the two o' ya out from in me, an' ya been nothin but humorless ever since.

MARGARET: But Mother, what we do is important. It touches people.

BILLY: She's right. A work like this connects with people. It helps them realize that their own families – ones they'd always secretly considered to be dysfunctional, but tried very hard to pretend otherwise – are actually completely normal, because in reality everyone's family is dysfunctional to some degree. Which ironically, and sadly for drama, makes the genre something of a redundancy. (*Beat*) Though I've a feeling I may have just undermined my own argument.

MOTHER: Look at ya – both o' ya – you're pathetic! You're both so stuck on some fancy idea 'bout the weight of what ya do that you've forgotten to have a good time. Well, old as I am, I ain't. (*Beat*) But…I will say this before I go. There's one thing this godforsaken piece o' crap's taught me. Somethin, now I think of it, that *is* pretty damn life-changin.

BILLY: I knew it.

MARGARET: What is it, Mother?

MOTHER: All them years ago, when ya Pa just up an' left me, right after he'd seeded me with a couple o' brain-dead tit-suckers that

91

made my life feel so much worse than it already was…well, I just plain hated him. I wanted him to die. But I realize now that he was right. Despite all the pain an' bitterness he caused me over the years, I can see now that he did what he had to. He was right to get out – to leave while he still could. He could tell what a big slab o' misery we were dumpin on the world, an' he wanted nothin more to do with it. And now – slow on the uptake as I am – neither do I.

(*MOTHER takes her cane and begins to pull herself up from her chair.*)

BILLY: Where are you going?

MOTHER: Ain't decided yet. 'Wicked' maybe. 'A Little Night Music' if the timings right. 'Drivin Miss Daisy' if there's one on somewhere. Not a musical, true, but still a dream vacation from this cesspit.

MARGARET: Mother, don't leave us, *please!*

MOTHER: Sorry, honey. I feel a song comin on.

BILLY: Mother, I forbid you!

MOTHER: Ya do, do ya? Well ain't that nice.

(*MOTHER begins to exit stage L.*)

MARGARET: Mother, *please!*

BILLY: Stop, Mother – stop!

MOTHER: Oh, it's stoppin. It's stoppin right now. The minute I walk off this stage, this whole sad, sorry excuse for a play ceases to be. Without me…ya got nothin.

92

MARGARET AND BILLY: (*In unison*) *STOP!*

(*As MOTHER slowly exits, perhaps whistling a show tune, MARGARET and BILLY look at each other in disbelief, frozen in tableau, as the lights fade down to BLACK.*)

END OF PLAY

TACKED-ON ENDING

TACKED-ON ENDING

CHARACTERS

ACTOR 1: An actor from the play you've just seen.

ACTOR 2: Another actor from the play you've just seen.

SETTING & TIME

SETTING: Backstage.

TIME: The present.

At rise: ACTOR 1 is discovered picking up his various belongings and putting them into a bag. Presently, ACTOR 2 enters from stage L., a backpack slung over his shoulder.

ACTOR 2: Heading out?

ACTOR 1: Yep…yep.

ACTOR 2: (*Scanning the room*) I thought I left my… (*Beat*) Huh…I guess I didn't.

ACTOR 1: What?

ACTOR 2: Oh, nothing. Just losing my mind, that's all.

(*Pause.*)

ACTOR 1: Great audience tonight.

ACTOR 2: Oh yeah, fantastic. Stellar.

ACTOR 1: Not like last night's.

ACTOR 2: *Oh*...oh, don't even remind me. What the hell was wrong with that lot? Miserable bastards.

ACTOR 1: Beats me. Still, tonight's made up for it.

ACTOR 2: Damn right – and then some. They were loving everything I was doing out there. How about you? Felt good?

ACTOR 1: Well...I mean...yeah...I mean...yeah...more or less. It's just that...

ACTOR 2: What?

ACTOR 1: Well...I mean...it was good, all of it, it just...well, just right at the very end, it just...something...it just felt a bit off, d'ya know what I mean?

ACTOR 2: Yeah, endings are tricky. 'Course, I'm not in the last scene, so it's not really my problem.

ACTOR 1: Well, no, and...and the thing is...well...I mean...I don't wanna sound arrogant or anything, 'cause I'm not, I mean, you know me.

ACTOR 2: Oh, yeah, no, no.

ACTOR 1: But it was definitely off, and the thing is, it usually is…and the thing is, you know, like…I'm not sure if it's me…or the play.

ACTOR 2: Huh.

ACTOR 1: 'Cause, I mean, you know…I'm a classically trained actor.

ACTOR 2: Right, right.

ACTOR 1: I mean, I've had private coaching from McKellen.

ACTOR 2: (*Taken aback*) McKellen?

ACTOR 1: Oh, yeah.

ACTOR 2: Well, that's certainly impressive.

ACTOR 1: Yeah, yeah – he's very good.

ACTOR 2: You don't have to tell me. (*Musing*) Fancy that, private coaching from Sir Ian McKellen.

ACTOR 1: Oh, no…not that one.

ACTOR 2: What?

ACTOR 1: Not Ian – John.

ACTOR 2: John?

ACTOR 1: Yeah, John McKellen. He rents one of those studios over on Gower Street. He's very good. Very, very good.

ACTOR 2: Oh…right.

ACTOR 1: Anyway, the thing is…I know my stuff, you know?

ACTOR 2: Yeah, 'course you do.

ACTOR 1: But just at the end – and I have no idea why – something just always seems to ring a bit…false.

ACTOR 2: Well, like I said, you know – endings are tricky things. Sometimes they just sort of lazily drift off, leaving everything up in the air; other times, they get wrapped up all too conveniently by a bus load of silly coincidences that leave you with the feeling that you've just been ripped off; and then other times…well, other times they just feel a bit…tacked-on, you know?

ACTOR 1: Tacked-on? How do you mean?

ACTOR 2: You know, like a…what's it called? A deus ex machina.

ACTOR 1: A what?

ACTOR 2: A deus ex machina. It's a plot device that writers use – presumably when they're at a complete and utter loss of how to finish what they started.

ACTOR 1: But what is it?

ACTOR 2: Well, it's, you know, it's where they suddenly introduce some completely unexpected event or person or whatever that changes the whole scenario in one fell swoop and gets them out of the hole they've dug themselves into.

ACTOR 1: Sounds like a bit of a cop-out to me.

ACTOR 2: It is. And I've a feeling that that, my friend, may well be your problem.

ACTOR 1: Huh. (*Ponders*) Yeah…yeah, you might have a point there.

ACTOR 2: Remind me, if you will, how the play ends again.

ACTOR 1: You mean you don't know?

ACTOR 2: Hey, shoot me – I forgot, okay? I'm usually outta here after my last scene. I've got better things to do than stick around here all night.

ACTOR 1: All right, all right. I was just surprised, that's all.

ACTOR 2: All right, so?

ACTOR 1: So what?

ACTOR 2: (*Impatiently*) How does it end?

ACTOR 1: Oh, well…well, in the very last scene, my character's been left all by himself, so he decides it's time that he should be moving on, too, so he starts packing up his stuff into a bag.

ACTOR 2: Right.

ACTOR 1: But then, just as he's doing that, the guy from the earlier scenes – the one everyone thought had left forever – suddenly returns.

ACTOR 2: Right, right.

ACTOR 1: So, you know, they get to talking about this and that, the audience, stuff like that.

ACTOR 2: Yep, yep, go on.

ACTOR 1: And then comes this revelation. Well, sort of a revelation, I suppose.

ACTOR 2: Which is?

ACTOR 1: That my character doesn't feel that good about his, you know…his performance.

ACTOR 2: Ah, now this is definitely starting to sound familiar.

ACTOR 1: So the other guy starts telling him that maybe his performance isn't the problem, but the way the play ends.

ACTOR 2: Yes, yes, it's starting to come back to me now.

ACTOR 1: So then the guy starts telling him about some ludicrous plot device that writers sometimes use when they don't have a clue how to end their play.

ACTOR 2: A deus ex machina!

ACTOR 1: Yeah, that's it!

ACTOR 2: And then he realizes that the play has one?

ACTOR 1: Exactly.

(*Pause.*)

ACTOR 2: So what is it?

ACTOR 1: What?

ACTOR 2: The deus ex machina?

ACTOR 1: Oh, yeah…well, you see, when the other guy – the one everyone thought was gone forever but who then suddenly returns – well, when he was making his return journey, at some point during his travels, his wife's psychotic lover had somehow managed to plant a bomb inside his backpack.

ACTOR 2: Oh, come on! Oh, now that really is a cop-out. How ridiculous is that?

ACTOR 1: Yeah, I…I had my reservations, to be honest.

ACTOR 2: And what? The bomb goes off and they both get blown to pieces in some sort of inane tragedy, is that it?

ACTOR 1: More or less.

ACTOR 2: Well…there you are, then. There's your problem.

(*A ticking sound is heard.*)

ACTOR 1: Yeah…yeah, I think you might be right.

ACTOR 2: I know I am.

ACTOR 1: By the way.

(*The ticking sound becomes louder.*)

ACTOR 2: Yes.

ACTOR 1: What's that noise? Is your backpack ticking?

ACTOR 2: Yes, I believe it is. Why do you ask?

ACTOR 1: Well–

> (*Suddenly the backpack explodes and they are both blown to pieces in some sort of inane tragedy.*)

END OF PLAY

ABOUT THE AUTHOR

From the Royal Court Theatre in London to the Playhouse Theatre in Tasmania, the works of playwright Andrew Biss have been performed across the globe, spanning four continents. His plays have won awards on both coasts of the U.S., critical acclaim in the U.K., and quickly became a perennial sight on Off-Broadway and Off-Off Broadway stages.

In London his plays have been performed at The Royal Court Theatre, Theatre503, Riverside Studios, The Pleasance Theatre, The Union Theatre, The White Bear Theatre, The Brockley Jack Studio Theatre, Fractured Lines Theatre & Film at COG ARTSpace, and Ghost Dog Productions at The Horse & Stables.

In New York his plays have been produced at Theatre Row Studios, The Samuel French Off-Off-Broadway Festival, Emerging Artists Theatre, The Kraine Theater, The Red Room Theater, Times Square Arts Center, Manhattan Theatre Source, Mind The Gap Theatre, 3Graces Theatre Company, Curan Repertory Company, Pulse Ensemble Theatre, American Globe Theatre, The American Theater of Actors, and Chashama Theatres, among others.

His plays and monologues are published in numerous anthologies from trade publishers Bedford/St. Martin's, Smith & Kraus, Inc., Pioneer Drama Service, and Applause Theatre & Cinema Books.

He is a graduate of the University of the Arts London, and a member of the Dramatists Guild of America, Inc.

For more information please visit his website at:

www.andrewbiss.com

Made in the USA
Monee, IL
14 July 2020